Tears of Rain in the Pandemic and a Physician

Tears of Rain IN THE PANDEMIC and a PHYSICIAN

Zeenat Chowdhury-Jackson,
MD, FACP,FACE

Charleston, SC
www.PalmettoPublishing.com

Tears of Rain in the Pandemic and a Physician

First Edition

Paperback ISBN: 978-1-63837-186-1
eBook ISBN: 978-1-63837-187-8

Author's email: admin@zeejjjlimitedcompany.com

Dedicated to all victims of COVID-19,
front line workers, and healthcare workers.

CONTENTS

Tears of Rain 1
Thank You to My Colleagues 3
Buy Me 5
Flowers of Tears in Pandemic 7
Every Time You Leave Me 9
Accommodation in COVID 13
Storage Box 2020 15
Dignity 17
What Is It? COVID? 18
Love 20
Nightmare of Time; COVID Has No Time 22
Layers 24
The Pirate Goes to Heaven without a Smartphone 25
In Time 27
We Never Leave; Tell Our Ancestors 29
Prayer for the Password in Pandemic 31
Trauma Surgeon 33
Tour Guide 34
My Cockatiel 36
Desire 37
Degraded Hippocratic Oath from COVID Unit 39
My New Generation 42
Real Estate Pandemic 44
Retirement in pandemic 46
Light-Blue Sunglasses 49
The Extension 51
Inner Look 53
I Don't Exist 55
Madness of Possessiveness in Glitch 57
A Letter from a Solider in a Pandemic 59

Misplaced but Not Lost in a Pandemic 61
Wish or Choose 62
I Will Still Search for You 63
Photographer, Painter in a Pandemic 65
Bubble.. 67
Beautiful Mind 69
Money.. 71
Empty Year 2020 73
Adapted, Face to Face, COVID 75
Profile 77
Once upon a Digital Dream at a COVID-Free Platform 79
Post-COVID Rehabilitation.. 82
Win That Bright Beautiful Day 84

Tears of Rain

It is you and your presence.
You gave me a heart that can feel every color of the universe,
You let me listen to the sound of silence.
You gave me a mind to imagine the light of infinity,
a vision that can see through the naked human soul.
My sense to sense insensible,
a taste that can test the power of serenity.
You have weakened my frozen soul of a thousand years,
you made me fall in love with my sorrow,
you gave me the strength to love the pain of my sorrow,
the rainbow of my solitude.
Tears of rain, no fountain, no stream, lake, river, or ocean.
You could not see the silence of oppression,
could not see evaporated dreams of freedom, equal justice.
Wash out the story of oppression, slavery, inequality, millions of years of my captivity.

Break the chain of inequality,
tears of rain, a ray of light, on the way.
Wash the core of sadness, wash the core of numbness to a Milky Way.

Thank You to My Colleagues

My ID, my tag on my toe, my dead body.
In my distress, in my realization…whom should I call?
No waves in the sea. Call the navy?
All ships are on the sea, but not moving.
Call the air force?
No airflow.
Airplanes are in the sky, only floating, no movement.
Call the army?
All roads are cracked from COVID-19 like an earthquake;
no vehicle can pass.
My dead body cannot pass to the morgue for burial.
"No one passes me!" COVID-19 screamed.
My blood is not flowing, frozen, like the inside of a cold storage. Below zero.
My open wounds are not oozing, frozen.
I saw you at my bedside;
your voice was my only hope during my sedation.
You were my warrior, angel of life.

You came to me every day with your saddened, sunken, tired eyes.
You fought for me at the front line without fear of death, fear of COVID.
Warrior of the pandemic,
Dead bodies kept stacking.
I saw you kneeling down, on your knees
I saw you at my bedside at the ICU, angel of God, you kept asking me to breathe, screaming for oxygen.
My isolation at the ICU *ended*; I am free.
My ID, my tag, was once on my white coat,
now on my toe, covered with a body bag.
I was once a warrior of the pandemic
Now my death certificate is waiting online for you to put "cause."
All my life achievements, all my board certifications, are still on the wall.
The cause of death, not the war of human civilization,
the cause will be COVID-19.
I was also a warrior, a warrior of mankind.

Buy Me

My journey of present, past, and unfolding future,
perception of present,
broken, bruised emotions.
A power of art,
power of magic, can turn all darkness into floating glitters.
Scar of wounds, power of my pen, turns them all to tattoos.
My bleeding, my power of absorbency, turned bleeding to blush.
My cry, like a melody, no human has ever perceived.
My sadness a soothing message of peace,
an unheard poem in my hard drive.
Buy me, read me,
my incomplete, my complete, my defeat,
my crowded thoughts of clouds in my rest.
My fear in unrest, my feelings from BC, AD,
my perceptions of the present.
Your questions, judgments, will try to know my very best intention.

I sold my emotions, my tears, to save myself, a unique psychotherapy.
Buy me with your infinity;
buy me with the portrait of your soul.
Scan me.
Buy me.

Flowers of Tears in Pandemic

Tears were rolling from our eyes all night,
rolling, drying.
All the death certificates were signed online.
Fighting with COVID,
we saw our defeat,
my defeat.
We all were tired.
Our tears of defeat.
I woke up in the morning by a wake-up call, a whisper,
my very favorite whisper at dawn from a million light years away.
I woke up and saw all the flowers sprout from my tears.
So many flowers
I could not carry.
The graves are real; ashes are real.
Life and death are not virtual or digital.
I traveled to the graves,
the absolute destiny of life no one can escape.
Death cannot be virtual or digital.

I carried the flowers of my tears.
I returned back to my duty from the funeral.
No one knows I did not buy those flowers;
only you know those were the flowers of my tears.

Every Time You Leave Me

You were all standing between earth and Heaven.
You told me many times about this moment.
They were all intubated, on propofol, sedated.
I did not know if they would wake up again.
I begged to my demon, "What do you want? My blood or my tears?"
We *can* give both. We have both; we are human.
Which one do you prefer?
I will give you what you *want*.
Let my friends either go back to earth or forward to Heaven;
they do not want this time between earth and Heaven,
this time between life and death.
They are bodies, laying there, isolated, only to see through the glass door.
Take my blood or my tears; I have both. Exchange this, my demon.
You decide where they will belong, Heaven or earth.
Let the ventilator go; let the time pass between earth and Heaven.

I was standing there, and I saw you with my soul.
There were tears still on the dead body, at the corners of her eyes, when I checked her reflexes and pronounced her dead.
There were no family members, only me, in isolation, I can see through the glass door.
Take my blood; take my tears. I have both.
Another unique transaction with the demon.
Decide where they will belong: Heaven or earth.
Let the time pass between earth and Heaven, between life and death.
I was standing there; and I saw you all with my soul,
through the "Closed 24 Hours" glass door.
There were tears on dead bodies
at the corners of eyes
when I checked your reflexes and pronounced you all dead,
There was no family, only me and dead bodies, in solitude,
silent, no machine, no high-flow *oxygen*.
They do not need anything anymore,
withdraw all tubes, feeding tubes, all lines, IV lines, arterial lines,
flat line. Free. Only silence.
It was a cloudy day but bright eventually.
In this pandemic, no one is around.
Every time you leave me, you take a piece of my heart. I bleed.
I decided to wear my very dark lipstick, my N95, and woke up again.

Every time you leave me, you take a piece of my
heart.
I cannot dictate or say, "Please do not do it again,"
because COVID decides whom he takes or whom
he leaves behind.
He brings me the death certificate of *our* best physician, *best warrior of death.*
I read her wishes to be laid to rest, she wanted to be
with the ocean.
They all whispered their last wishes. I will still wait
for you at every sunset and every sunrise.
Many memories, smiles, now withdraw all tubes.
I was standing in the hallway.
I screamed, "Every time you leave me, you take a
piece of my heart."
No longer my heart is quarantined.
No longer a lockdown on the left ventricle,
No longer a piece of my heart left to take or give.
You all left me, left me to bleed.
I was standing like a zombie,
coronavirus vaccinated.
I feel as though I am nothing but a COVID-vaccinated
zombie,
with my very dark lipstick and my N95.
Every time you leave me, you take a piece of my
heart, and left me here bleeding.
Now it is my sorrow; it is only mine.
I asked who suffered the most.
I asked who loved you the most.
My silence, it is only mine.
It is *only me.*

I will also wait for you at every sunrise and at every sunset, the same as your last line.
It is my sorrow now and only mine.
COVID 2020: the year of my isolation and my imagination.

Accommodation in COVID

When you walk slowly with your walker or cane,
it is a reminder that I left you behind.
When you came to me through the ramp,
you were searching for words to tell me the story.
You kept searching for words.
I had to rush to the next encounter; your ride was waiting.
I left you behind.
You were searching for words that day to tell me, "Thank you for the last time."
You walk slowly, you search for your words, and I left you behind.
You are connected to me through an ancient oath.
That day you wanted to tell me the culture changed due to COVID,
due to digital society, you are left behind the digital wall.
You could not connect to the new culture, telemedicine,
you could not remember the password.
I know all your numbers, all your electrolytes.

I heard the sound, a song of your heart. I know
each graph of your vital statistics.
The heart that I used to listen to on every visit is
now in silence, not in sinus rhythm.
Now I see a flat line.
When you walked slowly with your walker or cane,
I left you behind.
Today, desperately, I want to go back to that day to
say I did accommodate you in my conscious, in
my mind.
I could not accommodate you in my time.
When you walk slowly with a walker or cane, I
leave you far behind,
but I did accommodate you in my heart and in my
mind.

Storage Box 2020

My belongings,
my possessions,
I am standing in my extra space
with green windows, green shutters.
My belongings, I carried a long way.
I carried them from winter to summer to fall and to the next winter.
I carried them from the Pacific to the Atlantic,
my belongings, possessions.
Now all are detached.
Extra space—the space is just right.
It is compartmentalized.
Some thoughts are stored in boxes;
some emotions are stored in bins. Maybe I will have some time
to reevaluate or recalculate its capacity, my capacity.
It is my extra space, just like existence in a moment.
I color-coordinated the boxes for my thoughts and emotions,
but suddenly I became color blind.

I detached my thoughts, my emotions, to put away
in storage.
A sealed box, sealed jar, sealed bin, sealed bottle,
suffocating, no vent.
My jar of blue memories, it cannot be evaporated,
erased.
Cannot be deleted, dissembled, divided, like my DNA.
I am at the storage unit; it is lit up.
It is the space for my possessions, my belongings.
All are standing there: my bogeyman, my demon,
my witch, the ghost of my past,
laughing at me.
I felt so defeated; the space is climate controlled.
Belongings will be stored well,
detached from me.

Dignity

Your chain could not hold Dignity's weight.
The gravity won.
The life within Dignity in the extreme heat had evaporated.
The icy light in the extreme cold hid the path from Dignity,
You cannot embrace Dignity anymore, you cannot hold her.
Dignity fell deep down under the sea.
She tried to float desperately,
but the gravity won;
the chain is broken.
A sudden storm of human cruelty silenced her core.
Dignity could not be sheltered from the extreme cold with the blanket of kindness.
Dignity was not guarded in your core of courage.
Love cannot survive without dignity.
Love cannot exist without dignity; it is just a draft.
Death of dignity, death of love.
The chain was not strong enough.
Gravity won.

What Is It? COVID?

Is this a disease of the mind, or of the body?
Is this REM sleep, a dream, or non-REM?
What is it?
No test for it.
It defines what you say.
I search for answers
Search for a remedy
Tired, sore
Sedation helps
No pain but fatigued
Not weak
Can stand up straight but does not feel great
Is it a disease of the muscle or a disease of movement?
I listen to you
I listen to myself
I listen to the light,
I listen to the dark
listening, listening, for seconds, minutes, hours, days to years
Fatigued

What is the disease?
It feels like a bruise, but no apparent bruise,
No pain
Bruised in mind, bruised in body, bruised in emotions
physical therapy, aqua therapy failed
Fatigue
Shopping used to help
Shopping for a new soul
Is this a disease of the soul?
Something is missing, or someone stole.

Love

Capture love
send some bullets though love
But love is still dazzling, dancing at the twilight zone
Shoot again, no blood, no tears
only a dazzling ray came from the bullet
Lit up the whole universe
Love lives, love survives
Chain the love
Chain did not bind
Love remains free
Only bruised wounded body
Love lives
Love remains free
Put the love in a cage
Love flies, travel through cage
Love changes, love shapes
Love remains in the universe
Robot measures, evil plots
Love remains free,
lives in reality and unreal dream

Love cannot be chained;
love remains free.

Nightmare of Time; COVID Has No Time

It always feels like a haunting.
The same nightmare:
Waking up suddenly, the fear of being late at work.
Today is Sunday in my deep sleep, my day off.
Suddenly I woke up. Oh, I am late for work.
It is like sleepwalking.
Did the test for REM sleep.
Anxiety for so many years, decades of nightmares,
nightmares for years.
I struggle to finish a exam or calculation in my dream,
I struggle to finish the lines.
Late for work, late for flight,
train of journey of life,
I fight with time, my personality,
fighting my subconscious to be punctual, all the time
waking up by a nightmare of years.
Hypnotized, went down to my early years
The anatomy dissection room doors always closed at 7:00 a.m.
No entry for those who are late

or you will face the cane
I was never late for any events since then
Anatomy dissection room, my favorite class of all
Late nights with human organs preserved in formalin.
86,400 seconds of my days are passing,
like vampires, the ghost of the past
comes at late night with a chime.
Do not be late.
Life is all about time.
Pandemic was unpredicted.
I am punctual, predictable, and always on time,
but this pandemic, COVID reminded me over and over again,
death is unpredictable, and has no real time.

Layers

America, layers of colors like a rainbow at the horizon
Colors of the free
Layers of cake, chocolate, vanilla, and strawberry
Layers of subconscious like layers of standing strong mountains
Layers of ice cream, a unique mixture of taste, like a magic fountain
Layers of clothes, for climate control in winter or deep-down sea
America—the name is so dear to me, like a smile of turquoise,
Layers of sparkling snow on Christmas trees
America, layers of love, red, white, and blue
Soft and safe like morning dew,
Layers of my beliefs remain free in the land of free.

The Pirate Goes to Heaven without a Smartphone

Society worships, prays
every day, every single day
We have homes
we have temples, mosques, churches, synagogues
Why cannot we enter your Heaven?
Guard of Heaven: "You are all smart with your smartphones, you all play telephone,
I see you uploading stories in the news.
You are smart but cowardly.
You did not have courage to intervene.
I watched it all in the news.
I was reading those in cross communication, CC, or blind communication.
Her head was down, eyes were fixed, fixed to the ground.
It does not make sense in the six senses or in any sense.
You are all playing telephone, uploading for millions to see,
like free entertainment.
Decided she is a witch

burn her alive, stone her to death
degraded ashes, disseminated with joy by you."
A pirate with a dark background
A pirate whom you all call savage with no smartphone
A savage of the sea
Saved her from the circle of abuse
not the prince of my fairytale,
A pirate from the sea.
The guard of Heaven gave the key to the pirate to enter the Heaven,
forgave his past for one good mission.
The keypad of Heaven's door is made of compassion,
it does not need advanced technology, only emotion.

In Time

In time I will wait for you
I will wait in BC, AD, or in my century
Kindness will give a blanket in the winter, shade in rain or sun.
The same way in BC, ancient time of Hebrew, AD, or in Sanskrit
The love in kisses will remain the same with or without makeup
The body will wash away like makeup, will melt, evaporate like ash
Love and kindness of the soul will time travel, from one timeline to the next.
Human love will remain the same in digital, on canvas, in death or in life
Mountains flatten, oceans dry, continents vanish or merge
In the galaxy, shooting stars disintegrate
Human tears are colorless from the beginning of time, flow in love, in pain, in joy
the human emotion, tears remain the same in BC, AD, or the same in my time

It is not the flesh. It is my soul that will wait for you in time.

We Never Leave;
Tell Our Ancestors

We are the absolute, part of your absolute
We left but we always come back to you in a different form,
in a different existence,
We will never leave you,
we will always guide you from a distance, you will not know.
We are in your existence, very faded, but we never go away completely
Your artificial intelligence can simulate the image, but they cannot bring us back.
Our images are absolute and cannot be captured.
You can only capture the non-absolute things in your virtual reality,
which changes time to time.
We are your ancestors, we will sit here until the end of time; we are your absolute.
We are like tears of your memories,
emotional turbulence moves you forward to your destination.

We are your ancestors, soothing whispers to your left ventricle,
we are your deceased ancestors visiting at the most troubled times
We comfort you in the subconscious, like a guide when you lose your way.
Part of your absolute, we are implanted in DNA, we are the unconditional,
we are the ones who will never leave you in good times or bad times. We are in your DNA; we are part of your "absolute."

Prayer for the Password in Pandemic

How can I open the door of your Heaven?
My action, emotion, existence, in my past, in my present
It is not wish, unlimited
It is not choice, limited
It is a prayer, prayer for the password at my last day
The guard of Heaven's door, asked me to define myself
I had my shutters at different angles to shade your rays when I lost my way
Do I define myself today as a healer, as a mother?
Do I tell them I am beautiful and rich,
and I am a lover?
Do I confess at the door of Heaven: my sin, my defeat, or my shame?
How can I define myself to open the gate of your Heaven?
Do I remind you at the gate how many times I went to the temple, mosque, church, synagogue?
Do I comprehend myself?
I did not celebrate my birthday

I did celebrate you every day
Not a wish, not a choice, a prayer for a password at my last day
The Heavenly door will open for me if I can define myself, with a divine secret code for *me*
I defined myself at the gate of Heaven
my words, my actions, my existence in my conscious mind did not make anyone cry
I did not shed the tears of others.
He asked me to define myself one more time. Then suddenly he smiled,
the guard of Heaven.

Trauma Surgeon

Trauma will reshape you.
I cannot feel anything.
After a car crash, the Trauma surgeon asked, "Can you feel the pain, can you feel your limb?"
No, no, all numb, the answer no one likes to hear.
His hand was shaking,
only a trauma surgeon can save you at this moment.
Pain means a viable part of the body,
Pain means alive.
Pain is powerful, it will move you, shape you.
Pain will change the punishment to privilege.
It will reconstruct you, like a trauma surgeon,
give you a new look.
All reconstructed, typed up in a digital computer, like a digital book.
No one can reconstruct your past, even the powerful pain.
"You survived your past. Why do you want to go back or time travel to your past?"
Because in the past I was real, not digital, not reconstructed.

Tour Guide

My book was pretty, beautiful, but I could not remember the index.
I was walking at the sidewalk of a beach in Hawaii.
The whole sky looked like it was made of Pyrex.
Walking along with one hundred thousand people at Coachella, I could not remember the index.
I felt nothing to lose or conquer.
The tour guide arrived on time to take me to a carpet ride,
when I fell down from the Grand Canyon.
I felt I was pushed from the cliff of a mountain; I did not know why.
When I lost my path with pain, the tour guide taught me how to see the tears of rain,
and showed me how to travel through a soft dew when I am in pain.
The tour guide helped me learn how to listen to the sound of silence when everything became hopeless.
My unique transactions were all declined.

The tour guide does not fight with the conscious, it resides in the deep subconscious.
He took me to a carpet ride to calm me down,
took me to the year 1400, showed me who was burned alive, showed me the burning believers.
Why was Joan of Arc perceived as a witch?
He comforted me and took me to 6 BC.
Showed me the pain, the pain of being crucified alive.
The carpet ride, the tour was the index,
my overall strength to overcome isolation, my sorrow when it was intense.

My Cockatiel

Fly, fly, cockatiel, fly back to me
I do not want you to sleep alone in the grave
I want to carry the ashes with me wherever I go
Our cockatiel
Come back with beautiful thirteen years on your wings
The ashes once I wanted to give to the ocean
Now I want to keep the ashes close to me
I know now you are free
You will remain alive with all my blue memory.

Desire

Early morning

Flat tire
Desire to go to my destination
Desire for the wheels to move, for all green lights

Late afternoon

Raindrop, rain pouring
Desire to get wet in the rain, but was in uniform,
was on duty

Late evening

Late patient
Saddened with breast cancer without insurance
Saddened my day
Desire to give her insurance
Desire to cure her,

assure her,
Desire to see her back in my office with her smile
with highlights in her long hair, grown back after chemotherapy

Late night

At home, desire to hear my pet bird alive
Desire to hear her unspoken noise or sounds or language between the bird and my child.
Desire to see she is sitting on my daughter's shoulder
touching my daughter's cheek with her beak

Late midnight

Sleepless, late coffee
As if life insurance kicked in after death
Dying to write all night
Digital typing, digital feelings
Keep writing
It was so silent at night,
digital typing getting louder and louder
I looked for my quiet ink pen with my deepest pain
all ink was frozen and washed out with tears of rain

Degraded Hippocratic Oath from COVID Unit

Degraded Hippocratic oath in color-coordinated alert, code blue
It alerts us of our time of misery,
COVID craving human life,
thriving on human tragedy,
swimming in tears of human pain
there was no gain.
Boosting its self-pride, mocking our misery,
felt like a degraded Hippocratic oath in color-coordinated alert
How can you see my smile under my mask?
You felt my tears of sorrow from a glass door
the smile with difficult breathing, prayed for a Heaven without medication,
a Heaven without life support
one month, two days in the COVID unit.
In my very silent moment
In my deep realization of my life,
my only life
I was not able to breathe in my unpredicted agony,

in a very dark moment where I did not even know where I was going.
I was in isolation only with COVID.
It is the people whom I never knew that gave me the strength with their unconditional love.
I wonder why?
I am in debt now forever to each one of you
I do not call you every day,
I am unable to show my appreciation
I cannot give you anything more precious than what you have given me,
your everyday powerful thoughts for me to get my second chance
You all went to Heaven for me, and if there is a God, you stood in front of that powerful entity.
You brought that for me, my second chance.
I was powerless, sedated, I was incapacitated.
I sensed the strength of the powerful gift that God has given to the human soul.
I decided to cancel my flight to which I call home.
I choose to take a flight, very uncertain, to unpredicted Rome
only because of you.
If I ever cry with agony again or am shredded into pieces for the choice I made,
still I will tell myself only one thing: I stayed for you.
This the only thing I can do because
I do not have anything more precious than what you have done or given me.

If I give you more time, then I will not be on time
    for the next encounter.
A degraded Hippocratic oath in color-coordinated
    alert, code blue.

My New Generation

I am close to the finish line
my traditional conventional journey, like my daily morning coffee
my new generation said I never tried or dared to try anything nontraditional or nonconventional
your new wave of nontraditional unconventional,
sometimes I ignore or sometimes I do not understand
life of a mermaid
like the dance of tide, watching your journey
life of a mermaid, you feel the wave of ocean with your fin
you cut the waves with your mermaid tail
you said you want to stop the wave of sea for a moment; then you can sleep, countless waves,
life of a beautiful unicorn, said I am your dream
I asked you to hear the real sea, not the artificial waves
touch the sand under your feet, not the virtual dream on the computer screen
you know how to stop the waves to sleep

you swim in the waveless sea, with mermaid tail,
you can hear the unspoken words in the sound of silence, listen to the tears
Instagram, TikTok, YouTube, Twitter
all are digital platforms, a real awareness to hypnosis
the end of night, Da Vinci
I gave your name on your birthday
now millions of people see you blowing your magic candle
your digital platform is free of germs, but the community is unknown
up all night like a vampire party
I cannot make you to fall sleep with lullaby anymore.
You fall asleep at dawn,
birds, dew, flowers all wait for you all day at the arrival of a new day, but you have no day or night.
all climate controlled, no rain, no winter,
It is convenient, artificial, digital
It is difficult, difficult to wake you up to feel the real thing
like millions of waves, countless,
your followers, like dances of a tide or a TikTok,
like the life of a beautiful mermaid to me

Real Estate Pandemic

Oh, my oleander
Oh, my ocotillo tree
Your roots are embedded in my heart,
This is the year of twenty-three
I drive out every day
I drive in late, you blink
you blink at me with the light of landscape.
I looked at the garden I created from my imagination, which I did not buy
Now I have to leave, leave very far
Every real estate agent said there will be many oleander trees
Red, white, and pink
Granite countertops, window shutters, bay windows
Every real estate agent smiles. You will have a mansion of windows in your next home.
We will bring the ocean closer to you.
It is an investment,
it is like a profit.
Ocotillo, you were once a baby,
you looked at my crying eyes

like my mother once spoke out, "Go and explore your new garden;
there is always a way to come back to me if you wish or choose."
No, I cannot leave my oleander flowers, ocotillo tree
They are not for sale, or for profit. They will go with me.

Retirement in pandemic

My employment and twenty years of my life
Is this time bigger than twenty light years, the limit of my life, my only life?
It was my identity, my productivity, my ID badge.
As my employer you were there every day, in my Christmas, in my Thanksgiving.
Many things happened in those twenty years,
in each second, some were intended, some were unintended,
some were like accidents, some were just like luck, but all were accountable in my sincere consciousness.
I only counted my productivity, my ID badge.
That productivity is the sole purpose of human life, it is survival.
Some years I could not make the cut,
I got terrified in my dream for twenty years when I was at the border of homelessness,
between insurance or no insurance
My life insurance, my twenty years, all connected to my employment, my employer,

they know more about our story than any book can hold.
I have given you my twenty years of devoted mind, but you periodically evaluate my mind.
I was really insane not to look at all the beautiful mountains to rush to work on time every day, on time, every day on time, without my makeup.
Now it is too late to slide my time card again, too late.
Siri, Cortana, my iPhone remind my shift, my meeting, every morning, but they do not have a reminder of the end of my shift, like my retirement.
There were no reminder that I had to pick up my daughter's diapers, diapers for my elderly mother.
I gave the prime of my life to you.
My employment, my employer, you helped me to keep them warm.
I survived with you the recession of 2008 and pandemic of 2020;
I was sometimes complete, sometimes incomplete.
A sudden war of depression in 2008, when I had to write the most prescriptions for antidepressants for patients in my life combined,
Sudden war that caused limb loss, nowhere to run or crawl
Collapse of economy, human loss of security, loss of comfort of health and mind.
Sudden war between humans and an unknown virus,
A war between consciousness and subconscious,

A war with no real tank, but with an oxygen tank, ventilator, and the virus named COVID-19.
I survived with you the recession, depression of 2008, and pandemic of 2020,
My employment, my employer, validated my all insurance, licenses, privileges.
Today you will validate my retirement, journey to no badge.

Light-Blue Sunglasses

Light-blue sunglasses detect
the kindness from the shade of the palm tree
when there is tiredness from misery
The red-light sunglasses of perception where everything is perceived like red blood
like anger, distorted like Dracula
Dracula can see through all demons, demons can see through red-sunglasses
Richer and richest but you react the same way when I get sick.
Poor and poorest
The poor cries the same tears as the rich when suffering
All REM sleep are same,
We only differ in our perception
We are not robots
Robots analyze, diagnose, detect, compare, and graph with no perception
You are sent once as the most powerful, richest man on the earth
You perceive life in your way in an advanced society

You once came to the earth as a young, powerless girl at a street corner of the third world
To see her life with perception of humiliation, hunger.
She was repeatedly unjust by perception of society
The perception shapes the future
Sometimes destroys city after city
Perception created a human bridge of compassion
Perception made you sometimes a human or a demon

The Extension

Losing the extension, losing my contact list
Golden chain of my Louis Vuitton reflected to my eyes, saying "Open your eyes"
Golden cap of my Estée Lauder lipstick shined a light on my lips saying, Breathe
I was in the middle of the road, failed to make a left turn
The gold cover of my watch said, "Wake up, shining light, time to wake up"
The watch did not have an alarm, the watch was half broken
My silk red blouse was a designer one; I had to work hard for it,
it soaked with red blood.
I realized I was in a collision.
I searched my mind for my extension,
my phone, my iPhone, easily synced.
Searched for the prince of my fantasy to come rescue me, sync, or save me from my misery.
My extension, my contact list was crushed.
I desperately tried to remember the numbers,

I can remember her contact number even when
unconscious
I could not dial, but I saw she was right there, right
there for me
my unconditional love, my unconditional extension, the only one that synced.

Inner Look

Dreaming is a navigator; inner strength is a sailor of a stormy night
Outer looks fade away, but inner looks stay with us until the end of time
Outer looks are to win the outer world, to win cheers from others
but inner looks are to win yourself, to know who you are
Inner strength—you are the only one to understand, and cheer
It will give you the patience to wait in a very cold winter night for the next train,
the one that you missed after working late in Washington, DC.
It will give you courage to go back to work after being injured during your residency.
Inner beauty will give you the compassion to go back to comfort a patient, in an era where there was no specific treatment for HIV.
Inner strength will let you see through the glass door in the pandemic and accept your tireless defeat.

It is the weapon to fight against all the odds and to win.
Inner cores will fight through the preeclampsia and HELLP syndrome to give birth to a new life,
fight through the Great Depression, pandemic, defamations, reprimand, or failure of any certification.
You may not have a friend who will understand you or your inner look.
You are the only one to know yourself the best.
Every power lies within yourself.

I Don't Exist

No one has seen my wound, they said it was too dark to see
you did not see my tears, you told me you thought it was raining.
You did not hear my cry.
You told me you thought it was the sound of thunder,
It took a decade to write one poem
I was once on top of the mountain
I was able to see every groove of the mountain, rivers flowing
You all said my need is limited
I do not need anything more, I only need food and faded clothes
You dictated, decided a century before what I should think and dream.
You decided when I should breathe,
without my consent you all trespass me for centuries.
I was crying of pain.
You decided I do not need anything,

because anything will be more expensive than my pain.
Close the wound, close the wound
I said keep it open, keep it open, let it ooze, I do not need to hide
Let the wound drip and soak all the nerves to make everything numb
You dictated everything for me, every move of mine
It is not me,
I do not exist.

Madness of Possessiveness in Glitch

Like COVID-19, our distance will always define our wishes and choices.
I am frozen in a glitch.
My possessiveness defines the distance between us, like COVID, my glitch.
Moon: "I am a billion years old with my silvery rays, with my old heart, old in age and old in time.
My beliefs are dull. My silvery wishes, frozen in a glitch.
I will never be able to meet your expectations with a glitch.
I know I am beautiful until the end of time; you see me.
My flaws of possessiveness, I will not let you breathe without me.
Glitches are exceeding my breathing like COVID.
Dreams are unlimited. If you choose one, you will be limited;
you will cry out for space.

I will tell you I am your only space, I can share anything but I cannot share you like the last sip of my large coffee.
I want you to look at me, only me, until the end of time, my glitch.
My flaws only exist for you.
My IT, information technology—we are all digital, no paper, no canvas, a COVID-free platform.
My possessiveness defines the distance between us,
images disappeared from my inbox, like an in-patient list.
I searched in my iPhone, my pager, laptop and desktop.
I click and delete.
Sounds of clicks, glitches on my call day, post-call day, like post-COVID,
we have the same universe to share.
I am invisible when you are present—what a madness of possessiveness'.
Madness of perfection with fatigue.
A flaw, a glitch.
Madness of a digital world.
A glitch, try to delete it in a COVID-free dream.

A Letter from a Solider in a Pandemic

There will be a moment when you will want to scream your heart out,
but you have to remain silent.
There will be a moment when you will find yourself injured,
and you will want the wound to heal fast.
You have to accept that scar for rest of your life.
You recall the moment when you wanted to reach out, but you could not, for their sake.
There will be a time in life when you will be miserable.
You will want to escape but you have to stand up to fight to win the battle.
You will keep winning, and at one point, you will lose the time to find the real you.
You did not win, but you can always remember that moment.
Certainly, you will find the gift in all this, and will see unseen colors.
It will be the darkest night.
You will be tired, soaked with blood,

but that night will be over with the brightest sunrise of your life.
I am your soldier, and I am sending this message to you: the winning moment has the glory.
Losing the fight will give you the strength to rebuild for your next endeavor.
Every second of breathing has a meaning,
Even when we sleep or dream,
we refresh our subconscious for the next journey to the next struggle,
one moment to another.
I was soaked with fumes of the battlefield.
Although I miss the perfume of my century, I know this fume will defy my next destiny.
This letter is only for you because the struggle and sacrifice you made is the ultimate meaning of every second of your life, your identity,
the last second of your clock, eternity.
At the last second of my life,
I want to hear the song that was never heard.
At the last second of my life, I want to see the color that no human has ever seen or reached.
I want to experience the dance of my waves as no one has ever experienced or exceeded.
Yes, at the last second of my life,
I will embrace myself as a whole, and so will you, in your last time to succeed.

Misplaced but Not Lost in a Pandemic

The mind was misplaced but not lost, overwhelmed during the pandemic
Not lost like dementia, where everything is detached,
All senses are dulled when the mind is lost
It is not lost but misplaced, scattered
All senses are overwhelmed, not dulled
Fear everywhere, emotions hanging from the ceiling
Fear of losing everything
Haunted by ghosts from the past
It is just misplaced, it is there but not lost
Anxiety of losing everything, everywhere is fear
I could have lived from a suitcase all my life,
like a gypsy from the boats,
floating without fear of losing land
Just floating inside the bubble of moment after moment
No lifeguard around
It is the most breathtaking calmness holding the breath under twenty feet of water
I always find myself,
my misplaced mind there
Not lost, just misplaced

Wish or Choose

Wish with my fairy tale, with silvery wand
choose to set the alarm
wish to have no storm, beautiful bright day
but choose to pray for an easy day.
Choose kindness of life, but wish for a magic carpet ride
Dreams are unlimited, but choices create limits
I wish for a rare black rose,
but you choose to treat me by ordinary prose
My wishes are creative, innovations of my mind
I wish to fly in business class but
I end up choosing economy
Choose your life, but I wish for unlimited options of imaginations and light,
In my dreams of escape and hope

I Will Still Search for You

I still search and look for that soldier in my real world
and my unreal world
in my conscious and my unconscious
The solider with a heavy machine gun, who put it
down for me
I was alone, shivering in a winter night.
I was his enemy
His fellow man came and said, "She is our enemy"
He asked him to leave and asked me to scream with
fake pain
I was scared,
watchdogs were outside everywhere
I was in a small camp transit waiting to be trans-
ported
He came close and said, "Do not be afraid."
All night he did not sleep, he did not blink.
I asked him why he is guarding me, if I am his
enemy.
He said, "My war is not with you, or the unarmed
My war is between two powers and views"

He dropped me to the main camp and whispered
to me, "Be safe."
Whisper of my enemy.
We are all soldiers in a given situation,
the ultimate test of goodness is how we treat others.
I still search for that soldier
searching every corner of my universe.
He guarded, sheltered me, but I was his enemy.

Photographer, Painter in a Pandemic

When I called you, it sounded like an echo from another planet
Far away
When we met, we found out we are from another planet,
lost our way.
Planet under the ocean, the world of fantasy, imagination of creation
You put a beautiful smile on my lips,
painted my eyes like stars, can see through the darkness,
portrayed me as a mermaid.
You understood my language, even if it was unclear.
Both of our minds sometimes float in creative harmony.
We see things differently.
You transformed me into an amazing painting,
You keep painting the beauty of universe, bringing it to life with your brush.

I will keep writing and giving life to the emotions of the universe with my blue pen.

You perceived me in your beautiful mind, more beautiful than I could ever imagine.

Bubble

Bubble of imagination
A waiting point in transition
The bubble of life
Bubble of a moment
We're dancing
We're floating
They were putting me to sleep at midnight
They were waking me at dawn
They were my escape, bubbles of my imagination
They were flocking like birds
A strong, sudden storm
I was worried bubbles would fall on the ground
I was worried bubbles would dry in the sun
But the storm made it stronger to travel in time
Travel from moment to moment
The sun allowed the bubble to transform into reality
Bubbles of my imagination, tranquility, new beliefs
Dancing moment to moment
Year after year, century after century
The heart inside the bubble, bubble of color, floating like a soul out of my body

All the blue memories opens the eyes
The ghost of the past dancing
What is missing? The bridge,
The bridge between past and present,
A desperate split between real and unreal.
Push harder to move the bubble,
The movement of the bubble, stood in time
Streams of bubbles
Waves of bubbles
Stop the stream, you screamed
Stopped the waves, waves of bubbles
Chain the bubbles, chain the ideas
Veil the bubbles
The ghosts of the past do not let it cross to the next century.
A bubble of new beliefs freezes the movement
Windmill moving counterclockwise
A bubble in a moment, every moment has a date
A waiting point of transit for my new beliefs.

Beautiful Mind

I do not have anything, my society
No fame, may be defamed, pain
I do not have recommendations,
I do not know anyone in your planet
Invisible beauty
No fame, no frame, no dimension
My identity has to redefine
My name has to rename as if I am reborn again
I am reshaped, reconstructed, amplified, my hearing, my vision
What can you contribute?
What can you communicate?
Once upon a time, I was asked, "Whom do you smile for?"
The answer was, *for you.*
I celebrated many occasions, graduations, milestones
Today I will celebrate me.
I want you to come with me, to celebrate.
Today I will love myself for the first time.
I want you to love me with me.

Today I saw my beautiful mind online,
my beautiful mind for you.

Money

Money is the product of labor
Money is the product of productive time, unless you win a lottery
Money can change reality
Money can buy many things, but money can't define
money cannot change, birth, death, accidents
It can change perception
A false glow of reflection
Money is powerful; our lives revolve around it
It cannot buy time, it cannot change time
How did it get invented?
It differentiates.
It differentiates poor and rich.
The money dictates who will eat
but will never define or comprehend you
We chase it, we lose it
We will chase it again until we have it, until we achieve it
At the end we will not use it, and will not have much use for it

We may have plenty of it, can you comprehend it?
It is like a mystery, a mystery of mankind
Money changes the reality
Although it will not change the end result of destiny

Empty Year 2020

Empty, empty room
Losing the fight
Losing you
Tired mind
Flat lines
You told me you will leave all the mountains for me
You told me I will never be alone
I will have the blue sea
We once watched the mountains and sea together
You told me *I will always find you there*
We saw the mountain from the hospital window
You were on just two liters of oxygen
How many times did I find the room empty?
People were vanishing
Last night before leaving you, with my tired mind and body, I feared losing you
The extreme fear that you will be sedated soon and intubated
I was standing outside the glass door.
To show me your smile you took out your mask, CPAP

You were struggling with anion gap
I ran to the glass door the next morning, but the room was empty
You wrote that you had left all the mountains for me and the blue sea
Mountains cannot move, cannot cry
Change the color, gray, blue
I looked at those mountains when we were losing almost everything, but not Hope
Uneven grooves, uneven layers, unpredicted
You told me I can take chances on those mountains; they do not fall
You can lean on them when you are weak
They are like moments, my mountains, a blue sea like a blue passport of free
Silver tops of those mountains, like a navigator for a sense of purpose
The stars smile to see my progress from above
I am not alone, you told me I will always have my blue sky and blue sea
Waves flow, disappear, year was empty
Waves speed up gently
Tide dresses up for a dance, for a last dance,
but the year was empty

Adapted, Face to Face, COVID

I opened an account and then closed it.
I created an image and then deleted it.
I buy and dispose.
I was born but cannot say I do not die, I do die.
Face to face with COVID-19 was confusing but everything changes
I adapted in my mind; I adapted in my body.
All the sounds of the ocean, all the sounds of the thunder could not break the silence,
the silence of eternity.
All the light of sunrise, all the light of the galaxy could not reach all that was lost.
Color of my memory, color of the rainbow, color of my sorrow,
I imagined it and then I erased it.
I kept moving within a bubble of a moment, within a fragment.
I am standing in front of you with tears of rain with all my changes and with all my losses.
I was standing in front of 2020 with defeat.
I am standing today with win and gain,

with a rainbow after rain.
I am with you again, I am within a bubble of a moment, a bubble of a fragment.
I was in the Pacific, I was in the Atlantic, and now I am in you.
Fatigue of adaptations, fatigue of changes, but you are with me standing with tears of rain.

Profile

It was early morning
My birth was predicted.
My digital society was not happy
with a girl with no profile.
The profile was not much appreciated.
A girl with small feet that they have to feed.
A veil to protect her dignity, but treated her with no dignity.
My mother suddenly received roses from the queen because the prince was born on the same day.
Roses for all the newborn babies, new arrivals.
I was not an icon like the baby prince that saw many paparazzi in his room.
I was a baby girl with no profile, but had the same birthday as the prince.
One night a fairy came to see me.
She said, "I have wands on sale, sale for free."
I was confused with her words "on sale for free."
She approached me and said, "I have wands of love, wands of money, beauty.
Red, blue, and white, like the flag of the free,

you can have a profile, change your profile."
I asked her to give me a wand to change COVID.
She replied that she is from the land of the fairies.
They do not have any wand that works on COVID.
This is the end of the story of our reality.

Once upon a Digital Dream at a COVID-Free Platform

Was COVID stored for many years?
One day I woke up on one Sunday in a digital dream.
In a COVID-free digital platform.
Like COVID, I could not decide between stoicism and libertinism.
COVID-19 wakes up after thirty-five billion years,
like my childhood dolls, opens its eyes and then closes them.
The digital chip like COVID was preserved under a volcano,
Volcano erupted, tears evaporated,
Digital dream, digital sunrise, was singing a digital lullaby
Far away from the galaxy, captured by a digital web.
The web caused bruises in my dream;
I hear everyone saying I am a thief.
What I stole, I do not know.
I wrote a book; I sold the bruise as my beauty in a virtual store.

I escaped to a COVID-free home, to an enormous digital country,
a virtual gallery to complete me.
A book, a story of wind, that breeze over a question of human inability,
The pages of the book that veils bruises, hidden from all possible reality, digital or dream.
Thief, thief, I don't know what I stole.
Someone whispered, "You stole a digital character for your online book, virtual dream."
My imagination with gold and silver, it was not real, only a dream.
There was no real blood; it was just a glow of pain,
a judgment in reality for creating a digital character for the book in a digital dream.
I was standing surrounded by bars in custody in reality.
I asked the judge if I was in my unreal world, in my dream.
The judge asked, "Where is the digital character, book, surrender all dreams,
give those back, then you will be free."
I was ostracized, terrified. I wrote the book with imagination, created the character in the dream.
The judge asked to give back the digital character, the dream.
My dream is gone. I am awake in the reality. I do not have the dream.
I cannot bring the dream to reality.
I heard there is no punishment for human dreams, no punishment for dreams.

COVID does not exist in a dream, a COVID-free dream.
The judge gave me a punishment. In reality I will never be able to sleep.
Now I am a thief,
with sleepless nights.
I cried out. It was a dream; I cannot bring that digital character from the dream.
The judge again ordered, bring the digital character, the dream to reality, then I can be free.

Post-COVID Rehabilitation

I was pushed through the long, long hallway,
the hospital hallway where I stayed *fifty days.*
Pushed through the long rehabilitation, I stayed there *fifty days.*
I stayed with you fifty years.
I came home with a *nasal cannula*
Scar on my trachea.
I came through long, long hallway.
I pushed the society forward every day,
now I am dependent on Social Security.
Dependent on disability.
You all pushed me in a wheelchair.
I lived with you *fifty years.*
I heard once, shock her 300J, 360,
epi, epinephrine, and epi,
I remember I danced with you in my pretty black dress for 365 days.
Today I see at your face questions of uncertainty,
questions of struggle.
You keep looking at the ceiling all day.

I sense the struggle of feelings, struggle to love me again.
I pushed through long, long hallway, came long way,
but I cannot dance on my post-COVID days.
My soldier, trauma surgeon, tour guide, my tears of rain all together now to overcome.
I know I will dance again with the waves and my pirate of the sea.
My inner beauty has that promise to me.

Win That Bright Beautiful Day

My index,
My Pyrex sky, the mountains
Soldiers, trauma surgeon, tour guide, my inner look
are all here to fight for us
Are all here to move us forward,
fighting with COVID.
Fighting with our demon, a global struggle
All are with us, and my tears of rain today.
The pirate of the sea
Are all here for us,
with my sorrow
to win that bright beautiful day.

www.ingramcontent.com/pod-product-compliance
Ingram Content Group UK Ltd.
Pitfield, Milton Keynes, MK11 3LW, UK
UKHW020416250726
13967UKWH00007B/2674